DEATH DUTIES: THE CHEVRA KADISHA JEWISH BURIAL SOCIETY

What Being Around the Dead
Taught Me About Life

SALLY BERKOVIC

Death Duties:
The Chevra Kadisha
Jewish Burial Society

Sally Berkovic

© 2022 Sally Berkovic.

Creative Concept and Graphic Design: Gilad Visotsky • info@gilad-v.com

ISBN: 978-0-9552875-9-6

Published by Fishburn Books www.fishburnbooks.com

With thanks to The 13 Tammuz 5769 Trust for its support of the printing and distribution of Death Duties.

In memory of my beloved brother,
Eugene Berkovic, Ya'akov ben Eliyahu v'Chava
1964 – 2017

Dedicated to my husband Jonathan Fishburn:
his kindness and care is my everything.

And for my daughters, Avigayil, Elisheva
and Yonina: their zest for life fills me
with joy and hope for the future.

Death Duties is a work filled with tenderness, vulnerability, mortality and hope. It tells not only of losses, old and new, in a stark, unadorned and poignant way but also how personal grief can be transformed into a thousand anonymous kindnesses to others.

Dr. Erica Brown,
Vice Provost for Values and Leadership, Yeshiva University
and Director of the Lord Rabbi Sacks-Herenstein
Center for Values and Leadership
Her latest book is Esther: Power, Fate and Fragility in Exile.

In this boldly rendered, beautifully illustrated essay, combining profound wisdom and crisp, often humorous writing, Sally Berkovic invites her readers to join her in "normalizing the conversation around death." Beginning with an explicitly imagined description of the ritual ministrations to her own dead body, Berkovic draws on her personal and family history, her extensive knowledge of Jewish sources and traditions, as well as her up-to-date understanding of today's COVID-complicated zeitgeist - all to inspire, educate, and advise on a wide range of death-related matters. A sorely needed contribution to a topic that affects us all.

Judy Klitsner,
Senior Lecturer at the Pardes Institute of Jewish Studies
Author: Subversive Sequels in the Bible: How Biblical Stories Mine
and Undermine Each Other.

Contents

About This Work

Death Duties has its origins in 'Six Feet Under,' a talk I gave for the JDOV [Jewish Dreams, Observations, Visions] series in 2015, sponsored by the Pears Foundation in the UK. I shared my observations about my work on the Chevra Kadisha, the Jewish Burial Society. *Death Duties* expands that original text, reflecting on personal bereavements, life-saving surgery and the impact of the COVID-19 pandemic on our death and mourning rites.

My immense gratitude to Rabbi Shoshana Boyd Gelfand for offering me the opportunity to participate in JDOV: the original talk can be seen at jdov.org/talk/six-feet-under/

Questions to Consider

I hope that *Death Duties* helps facilitate the important conversations about one's own death and legacy that are often difficult to initiate with family and friends. Although it focuses on Jewish rites, the issues are universal, and you might find it helpful to use the questions at the end of *Death Duties* to guide your significant conversations.

A Matter of Jewish Law

Death Duties does not offer halachic – Jewish law – guidance, although it is informed by Orthodox practices. While my experiences give the reader a general overview of the Chevra Kadisha and the Taharah, the ritual cleansing process prior to burial, it's likely that there are slight variations and local customs practiced by the Chevra Kadisha in your community.

There may also be sensitive situations requiring certain adaptations. Please consult your local rabbinic authority for specific advice.

Acknowledgements

My appreciation and thanks to the following who generously offered many helpful insights: Dr Elliot Jager, Dr Leya Landau, Lisa Clayton, Doreen Samuels, Dr Elana Sztokman, Adam Taub and Daniel Taub.

I am deeply grateful to Dr Erica Brown and Judy Klitsner who kindly agreed to offer their approbation.

Special thanks to Gilad Visotsky for his inspirational graphic design.

The English translation of Kaddish is based on the Prayer Book for the Jewish Members of the HM Forces, Office of the Chief Rabbi, 1940

About Sally

I was born in Australia and am the daughter of Slovakian Holocaust survivors. I grew up in Melbourne and lived in Jerusalem and New York before an epistolary romance brought me to London. Since 2009, I have been the CEO of the Rothschild Foundation Hanadiv Europe, supporting Jewish heritage and culture.

My first book, Under My Hat was published in 1997 and short-listed for the Jewish Quarterly Prize. It is a social commentary-cum-memoir focussed on the challenges of raising daughters while straddling the tensions between an Orthodox religious life and the competing forces of secularism. Updated and reissued in 2019, the book explores the impact of more than 20 years of evolutionary change, including women's scholarship, Orthodox women clergy, enhanced ritual participation and women's political and communal leadership.

Visit sallyberkovic.com to read my blogs
and listen to my BBC2 Pause for Thought broadcasts.

I'd be delighted to hear from you about your own Death Duties. You can contact me via the website or by email - sally@sallyberkovic.com

יִתְגַּדֵל

וְיִתְקַדֵּשׁ

שְׁמֵהּ

רַבָּא.

Magnified
and sanctified
be His
great name.

My Burial

I will lie on a cold metal table. A sheet will cover my still, naked body. It is a body that no-one, other than my husband, has ever seen. It will be tranquil in the room. Four holy women of the Chevra Kadisha, the burial society, will wash their hands, dry them with paper towels and pat their splayed palms with talcum powder. This helps to slide on the two sets of latex gloves they will wear. In a quiet murmur, each one will say the designated blessings for the task ahead. No words, other than brief instructions, will be said. And so will begin the preparations for my burial.

A simple pine coffin sits on a raised trolley in the room. It will be filled with some sawdust. Some earth from the Land of Israel will be sprinkled on top of the sawdust. If I cannot be taken to the Land of my Ancestors, at least some of the modern miracle of the Jewish State will sanctify the ground and accompany me wherever I am buried.

A couple of small padded cotton bags will be placed in the coffin as a pillow for my weary head that will sleep for a very long time. They don't know I get a sore neck from pillows. A label will be placed on the coffin with my name. Sally Berkovic. Sarah Bat Eliyahu. Sarah, named after my father's mother murdered at Auschwitz. Sarah who never met her grandchildren or her great-grandchildren.

Now I am Sarah. Sarah, the daughter of Eliyahu, who died before he could meet his granddaughters. Eliyahu, whose name, as is common in Jewish families, lives on through his descendants, through my daughter, Elisheva.

Death's Bureaucracy

The women will remove any vestiges of death's bureaucracy – a name tag from the hospital, perhaps remaining bandages or tubes. They may nod at the long vertical scar down my breastbone attesting to my own brush with death when I had heart surgery in 2017. They may note the complementary scars on both legs and in the groin area. Although curious, no-one will comment, for it would be disrespectful.

As I lie flat, one woman will stand on my right side, another on my left and the third behind my head, gently supporting it lest it rolls. The fourth woman will ensure things are done correctly and pass relevant instruments to the others at the right time. Three women will delicately lift the sheet, stand behind it, and the fourth will pull at a strategically placed shower head and spray me with water from my head to my toes as I lie on my back. Keeping my modesty preserved is considered a sacred act and so the sheet will be draped back onto my body. Whenever it does not need to be exposed, my body will be covered.

Then the woman on my left will heave my body over to the right side and one of the other women will take the shower head and spray me with water as I lie side on. The water will pass over my hair and my face. My arm will be lifted so the water reaches under my arms and trickles onto my breast. The water will continue to drizzle to the tips of my toes. The process will be repeated as they heave my body to the left side.

Lying flat again, and covered as much as possible, the woman on my right will clean the nails on my right hand and foot. On my left, the woman will clean the nails on my left hand and foot. My hands and feet will be quickly washed again. The woman standing by my head will gently comb my exposed hair. Any stray strands of hair will be collected and put in the coffin. She will remove any detritus still in my mouth or nostrils. The wet sheets that have been covering me will be thrown to one side and immediately in its stead, a clean dry sheet will be put over me again. The women will all ritually wash their hands again and don a fresh set of gloves.

A vat of rainwater is perched on a specially designed contraption above the metal table. Now that I have been physically cleaned with tap water, I will be ritually cleaned with the rainwater, the same sort of water that filled the *mikvah*, the ritual bath, that I used every month during my marriage, except for when I was pregnant and now after menopause. Once again, three women will take the sheet off me and stand behind it. The woman standing at my head will release a lever that will tip the water onto my head. Holding on to the handle of the lever, she will slowly walk the length of my body ensuring that the rainwater spills out of the vat and covers all of me. Where there is no machine, buckets of rain water are filled and then emptied over the body. A short prayer will be said, closing with the words.

Taharah. Taharah. Taharah.

Pure. Pure. Pure.

Dressed for My Funeral

The *tachrichim*, simple white shrouds with no buttons, zippers or fasteners, have been used for nearly 2,000 years. In Talmudic times, Rabban Shimon ben Gamliel observed that the custom of dressing the deceased in expensive clothing put such a terrible burden on the relatives of the deceased, that they would 'abandon the body and run.'[1] Therefore he initiated the use of these shrouds so that rich and poor would be dressed alike. The woman on my right side will put my right leg through the right trouser pant, and then the woman on the left will put my left leg through the left trouser pant. And for the first time in years, I'll be an Orthodox woman wearing a pair of trousers.

---

1 Talmud, Moed Katan, 27B

A mask with two thick strings attached will be placed on my face and the strings will be wound behind my ears and then brought together in a bow under my neck to hold it in place. A bonnet will be placed on my head and tied securely into place with a little twist. Some grains of earth from the Holy Land will be sprinkled on my eyes. A shawl will be placed around my shoulders and the ends of it will come together near my breastbone. Near my breasts that fed my children many years ago. Near the breastbone that was ripped asunder to save my heart from expiring prematurely.

In fashionable layers, a simple, long tunic will cover the trousers and an apron-like piece of clothing will be placed around my stomach. A long belt-like strap will be taken behind my back and brought together again at the front. The women at each side of me will work in silent harmony to make a tight knot with the straps near my belly button. They will twist the knot three times and say *Aleph, Bet, Gimmel*, the first three letters of the Hebrew alphabet. Then they will start to make the three-pronged Hebrew letter called *Shin* with the straps. *Shin* for *Shaddai*, a name of God. God will be with me, like an umbilical cord attached to the world-to-come.

I am ready, and it is time to be placed in the coffin. The coffin is aligned with the metal table. On the count of three, the women lift my body slightly and glide it into the coffin. A sprinkling of earth from Israel is placed on my hands, my feet and heart. With great sensitivity and in unison, the women ask out loud for my forgiveness in case they upset me during the purification process or while dressing me in the shrouds. And finally, they put the lid on the coffin.

Time to be Buried

The mourners start to arrive – I don't expect a large crowd. Hopefully, my husband has predeceased me because I could not bear the thought of him grieving for me. I pray my daughters will have their own families and friends around them for support. The rabbi will invoke the prayers and then deliver the eulogy – a eulogy I will have written because I know exactly what I want to be said. We will all walk slowly towards the gravesite, but I will have the advantage of lying down.

Spades rest next to the mounds of dirt on either side of the grave. I am carefully placed in the ground, six feet under. My children shovel dirt onto the coffin, filling up the pit. There are some tears and quiet mournful sobs. My daughters look at each other and nod in agreement. They know that I expect this much, and so they start to say the Kaddish, the mourner's prayer...

Yitgadal Ve'yitkadash Shemei Rabba

And the only answer is *Amen*

בְּעָלְמָא
דִּי־בְרָא
כִרְעוּתֵהּ.

וְיַמְלִיךְ מַלְכוּתֵהּ,
בְּחַיֵּיכוֹן וּבְיוֹמֵיכוֹן וּבְחַיֵּי
דִּי־כָל־בֵּית יִשְׂרָאֵל,
בַּעֲגָלָא וּבִזְמַן קָרִיב.
וְאִמְרוּ
אָמֵן.

In the world
   He created
      according to His will.

May He establish His kingdom
during your life and during your
days, and during the lifetime of
all the House of Israel, speedily
and at a near time,
            and say: Amen

Funerals Denied

My Father's Story

In April 1944, during the Passover holiday, the Jews in my father's village were rounded up and taken to a ghetto in Uzhorod. After six weeks, they were deported to Auschwitz in cattle trucks. News of the horrors of Auschwitz had not reached their tiny village, so they had no idea what was in store. My father was one of four children. Upon arrival at Auschwitz, he and his older brother were sent to one side and tattooed with Auschwitz numbers. Their younger siblings, Rivka and Yakov and his parents, my grandparents Samuel and Sarah were never seen again. This happened on the second day of the Shavuot festival in 1944, the date my father [number A10927] and uncle designated as the *Yahrzeit*, marking the anniversary of the deaths of their parents and siblings.

After the war, my father and his brother went to Australia. Neither spoke of their experiences when I was growing up, however, at my father's shiva in 1992, his brother – my uncle – started to open up. He mentioned my father and their shared experiences in Auschwitz,

Right to left: Holocaust survivors - my father, Ted and his brother Alec and 2 friends, shortly after arriving in Australia from Europe, 1940s

and especially during the infamous Death March. And then he barely stopped talking about it till his own death in 2015. I often felt that talking about his experiences was finally a relief for my uncle, but also an obligation that he felt to the next generation.

In keeping with Ashkenazi Jewish tradition, I am named after a deceased relative, my paternal grandmother. Although anglicised to Sally, many in my generation were given common Hebrew names such as Sarah, Rivka, Rachel, Leah, Abraham, Isaac and Jacob, the Biblical matriarchs and patriarchs that were familiar names in pre-war shtetl life. The Bible was brought back to life in the naming of a new generation less than 20 years after the end of the Holocaust.

It was only as an adult that it dawned on me that when my grandparents, and indeed millions of others, died in the fires of Auschwitz-Birkenau, Treblinka, Belzec, Sobibor, Chelmno and Majdanek, there was no Chevra Kadisha to tend to their deaths. There is no cemetery or polished tombstone to visit on their *Yahrzeit*. Although I have been to the sanitized Auschwitz, I cannot make a meaningful physical pilgrimage to their burial site. The Nazis not only took away life, but at the same time, they also took away the mourning rites and the opportunity to grieve. This legacy finds mass graves still unmarked to this day and a children's park on the edges of the BabiYar ravine, a short train ride from downtown Kyiv.

My Mother's Story

My mother arrived in Australia in 1949 as a 12 year old girl and she never talked about her childhood in Slovakia. Occasionally I would try and ask for details but I was met with stony silence. Now I'm not sure if she wanted to talk, but sensed I was not ready to hear her story, or she had made a vow never to utter a word. However, in shielding me from her emotional wounds, I lacked an insight into my mother's psyche. It is only as an adult that I have begun to understand how the impact of loss defined her life. Now, I fear I have repeated this pattern with my own children because I too, have largely shielded them from my feelings of bereavement, albeit they are not comparable to the devastation my mother experienced.

Recently, I have increased clarity about the impact of this loss on my mother, myself and my daughters, and it comes in unexpected ways. For example, I had my own *Schindler's List* moment. No-one who has seen the 1993 Steven Spielberg Shoah film can forget the final scene where those saved by Oskar Schindler, and their descendants walk past his grave in the Catholic cemetery on the southern slope of Mount Zion in Jerusalem, pause and tenderly lay a memorial stone. My *Schindler's List* moment happened in Bratislava in 2018, timed to coincide with International Holocaust Remembrance Day on the 27th January, the anniversary of the 1945 liberation of Auschwitz-Birkenau. A public ceremony has been instituted to honour Slovak families who rescued Jews during the Holocaust. There I was in Bratislava, as members of the family who saved my mother and grandmother received a Righteous Among the Nations[2] award from the Embassy of the State of Israel in the Slovak Republic.

Each of the nine families being honoured have their own story, but within each intimate retelling, there is the epic novel of the Jewish people. My account started with an email in March, 2014.

> *My name is Pavol Krásny. I read your story on the site.[3] Very impressed me. My mother told me a story about a Jewish family that hid during the war in our house. (Scherer street 39 in Piestany). It was Mr. Arpad Weiss and two women. One lady died during the war. They were very harsh times. On the street marching German soldiers. Hiding in the house of a Jewish family was very dangerous. After the war, our friends went to Australia.*
>
> *Well, there are those times behind us. We believe that the suffering we will not have to experience.*

---

2 https://www.yadvashem.org/righteous.html
3 Pavol was referring to this website: www.furststory.com/English/YaldutBlum.html

I am glad that I managed to get your contact. I wish you good luck in life.

Pavol Krásny

P.S. Sorry for my English

My grandmother was one of those women, and her twin sister was the 'lady died during the war.' The email was sent to Naftali Furst, my grandmother's nephew, the author of the website in the email mentioned and whose life was documented in the film Kinderblock 66.[4]

Righteous Among the Nations

Clearing out his elderly mother's home, Pavol found a photo of a young girl he did not recognise. He attached the photo to his email, explaining that his mother told him about the family that her parents hid and that she remembered the little girl. That girl was Eva, my mother. By the age of seven, she had already been separated from her mother and hidden in several places before she was brought to Pavol's family home in 1944.

Shortly after that email, Naftali and I met in Bratislava. We travelled to Piestany to meet Pavol and Emilia, his 92 year old mother, the keeper of our memory. Many tears were shed that afternoon at Scherer Street as Emilia recalled our family: Janka Blum, the matriarch and her five children – Margit [Naftali's mother] Lily [my grandmother] and her twin sister, Anna who was married to Arpad Weiss, and two brothers, Rudi and Michi [see photo overleaf]. And after the tears, came the secret hiding spot, a small underground cellar accessible via a trap door, through which Emilia or her parents provided food.

Determined to ensure that Emilia's parents, Peter and Anna Brezovsky would be recognised by Yad Vashem as Righteous Among the Nations, Naftali started to collate the requisite proof. The basic conditions for granting the title include saving a Jew from the threat of death or de-

---

4 http://www.kinderblock66thefilm.com

This is the photo of Eva, my mother, that Pavol found in his mother's attic.

portation to the death camps, risking one's own life to do so without reward and personal testimony or documentation confirming evidence of their actions. The Brezovsky family met all the criteria, and four years later, we found ourselves in Bratislava again.

At the ceremony, the auditorium was full of the descendants of these rescued Jews, but instead of stones on a grave, there were warm embraces and pensive stares of wonder. Nine family groups were seated in clusters – the rescued, the rescuers and their respective descendants. Unfortunately, Emilia had died since we met a few years earlier. Still, Pavol brought his wife and children and I came with one of my daughters. A mini-documentary was shown about each family's war time experience using personal footage, archival and news materials and where possible, interviews with the ageing rescuers and the rescued. Each story involved the basics of survival, food and shelter, offered at great personal risk. A family representative came on stage to receive the award, and if there was a living survivor, he or she was invited to the stage to address the audience. I cannot stop thinking that I am alive because a woman made a dangerous choice to hide my mother.

Family Blum
(from the left)

Back row:
Rudolf, Margit,
Michi.

Front row:
Janka, Anicka,
Lily, Isadore

During that afternoon, I recalled an experience in 1992, when I spent a few days in a facilitated group encounter in Boston between the children of Holocaust survivors and the children of Nazis. My overriding memory is that most of the Jews felt sorry for the Germans, offering comfort and reassurance that they were 'good' Germans who bore no responsibility for their parents' or grandparents' actions. Burdened by shame and guilt, it was as if these Germans needed to prove to themselves, and to others, that they had not inherited the corrupted DNA

that drove their parents to do unspeakable acts. However, the prem-
ise was absurd. I could no more absolve them than they could take
responsibility for their forebears' actions.

Inherited Trauma

Inherited trauma, the idea that the emotional trauma of parents may
change their children's biology, has been used to explain the psychological difficulties experienced by some children and grandchildren
of Holocaust survivors. Beyond any possible biological impact, one
wonders how mere proximity to the traumatised older generation
expresses itself. For some, it is severe anxiety, depression and stress.
In my case, it manifests in doubts about self-worth – for what purpose
was I born when so many others could not be? Finding the answer is
what keeps me awake when I should be asleep.

Scanning the room of the rescuers' descendants in Bratislava, I wondered, could they too be harbouring inherited trauma? Knowing of the
bravery, risks and sacrifices made by their parents and grandparents,
are the next generation at risk of self-doubt and insecurity? Are they
paralysed by fear? Are they prone to existential doubt about their
mission in this world? Could the burden to be good be too heavy to
bear? Have they inherited the genome of kindness and altruism that
will ensure their actions are all ethical and moral, no matter
the circumstances?

After the formal ceremony, we were invited to the reception area.
Family groups clung to each other. Those elderly rescuers could still
converse with those they saved. They share a language – not only of
sounds, but also of memories. But the descendants? The words dimin-
ish with the generations. We are speechless. We smile. We pose for
photos that mask the trauma of our respective families. We create an
image that to the untrained eye suggests closure, that lulls the viewer
into believing that there's been a happy ending.

But the photos we create of the present also reveal the absent: those who did not survive, and their children who were not born.

In my family's story, there is much sadness for these unknown losses, but there is also gratitude. Lily, my maternal grandmother had four siblings: her brother Rudi was sent to Cairo in 1935 but he returned to Europe in 1939. Captured after fighting with the partisans, he was eventually deported to a death camp but the family have scant information. Her sister Margit and her husband took their sons, Naftali and Shmuel to Israel. Her brother Michi established a family in America. Both now have scores of descendants. Her sister Anna was married to Arpad Weiss. My grandmother's first husband who was my biological grandfather, died in the Ilava concentration camp on some unknown date. They had a daughter, named Eva who was my mother. Anna died while she was hidden during the war and was buried in Piestany. After Anna's death, Arpad then married Lily and together with Eva, they came to Australia in 1949 where they built a life together amongst a community of Holocaust survivors.

My parents married in 1959... yes, 1959. Less than 15 years after the end of the war. It's only recently that I've appreciated the magnitude of that act. Less than 15 years after the depravity of Auschwitz, my father had a suit, a job and enough psychological strength to imagine a future filled with love and children. My father did not have a sliver of self-pity, and I often recall his mantra, 'this too will pass.' Life taught him that indeed, everything does eventually pass...or die. He only had gratitude for the opportunities, safety and kindness Australia offered and never understood my wanderlust, particularly when I wanted to travel to Europe.

Struggling to think of an appropriate gift to bring Pavol, I decided that a few photos of my family might be appreciated; a snapshot of Lily and Arpad on a Melbourne beach, a posed photo of my parents' wedding and a picture from my brother's bar-mitzvah. Pavol smiles. His children look on as I point to a photo of five vibrant young women, each one pursuing her own passions. Three of them are my daughters, and the other two are my nieces in Australia, my brother's children. They are, I gesture, the five wonderful grand-daughters of the little girl that Pavol's grandparents hid in their cellar.

They are the future that no one dared to imagine.

My grandfather, Arpad, grandmother Lily and mother Eva
in their first home, Melbourne, 1950s

Let
His
great
name
be blessed
for ever
and to all
eternity.

יְהֵא
שְׁמֵהּ
רַבָּא
מְבָרַךְ
לְעָלַם
וּלְעָלְמֵי
עָלְמַיָּא.

little about the women. Luckily, I didn't sign up looking to expand my social circle. Occasionally, I see one of them at a community event or at the kosher supermarket. We might nod at each other in quiet acknowledgement, but more often than not, we barely recognise each other out of context. When we come together to perform a *taharah*, we hardly talk as it feels inappropriate to engage in casual banter. We all belong to an Orthodox synagogue as that is the basic criteria for being accepted into this particular Chevra Kadisha. While I sense that there is a spectrum of observance amongst the group, our individual differences are irrelevant for it is wonder and humility in the face of death that binds us.

As the *taharah* process draws to a close, I'm asked if I would like to do one small thing. I am encouraged to make one of the special knots that secures the garments in place. I nervously did the task, and considered that as my initiation into the Chevra Kadisha. It felt like their way of acknowledging my presence in the room, and allowed me to partici-pate in the *mitzvah* which showed great generosity of spirit.

The observation is designed to give someone the option to opt-out with no hard feelings, and a couple of days later I received a call to check how I felt about the experience. It did not deter me at all. In fact, it convinced me that this task was my destiny. The Chevra Kadi-sha operates every day other than Shabbat, and Sunday became my regular day. On my first official Sunday, women who had been doing this for 10 to 20 years welcomed me as the newbie and encouraged me to ask any questions. The day after, one of the women called to 'check-in' with me. Was I OK? Did I find it traumatic? Was it emotionally too difficult? This level of pastoral care is both reassuring but also an excellent professional protocol.

I have yet to deal with a baby or teenage suicide – I would like to think there's an expert Chevra Kadisha team engaged for such par-ticularly heart-wrenching situations. Women in their 50s have been difficult enough – knowing it could have been me and wondering why it hasn't been me.

A Secret Society

When I joined, I was instructed that participation in the
Chevra Kadisha should not be discussed publicly. It was simply something that should not be talked about. I did not query this requirement, and liked the idea that the Chevra Kadisha was not something
to publicise. It was a sobering lesson in subsuming one's ego as participation in this rite was not about drawing attention to oneself, but
rather was solely about the dead person. I was reminded of the morning prayer that lists those things for which we earn no reward in this
world, rather the reward is waiting for us in the World to Come. They
include honouring one's parents, visiting the sick, welcoming guests
and accompanying the dead to their grave. Acts involving the dead are
referred to as a *chesed shel emet,* an utterly altruistic deed, for there is
no possibility of reciprocity.

For several years, I was obedient and didn't tell anyone that I was
involved in the Chevra Kadisha and barely mentioned it at home.
However, a conversation with an American woman over Shabbat
lunch completely changed my perspective. I don't even remember
exactly how it came up in conversation, but she just started talking
about her involvement in her local Chevra Kadisha. I was shocked that
she was so open and without telling her of my participation, I gingerly
said something along the lines of 'how come you're talking about it so
openly? From what I've heard in the UK, it's not something you talk
about and there is a very strong ethic of keeping it hidden.' A man at
the table contradicted me, 'I'm involved in our men's Chevra, and no-
one ever told me not to say anything.'

Silencing women is a pursuit enjoyed by many, however my American acquaintance was not going to be quiet. She was not showing off
either - she was simply sharing the facts, highlighting the mitzvah, like
any other that we should all strive to do. She made the very sensible
point that it needs to be discussed so that people will join. It needs to
be addressed because it is a beautiful rite that encapsulates life and

death in one embrace. How can a community ensure the continuation of the Chevra Kadisha if it is clouded in mystery?

I was struck by the remarks of retired U.S. Marine Corps four-star general John F. Kelly about what happens to military personnel killed in action overseas – a protocol most civilians know nothing about:

> *Their buddies wrap them up in whatever passes as a shroud, puts them on a helicopter as a routine, and sends them home. Their first stop along the way is when they're packed in ice, typically at the airhead. And then they're flown to, usually, Europe where they're then packed in ice again and flown to Dover Air Force Base, where Dover takes care of the remains, embalms them, meticulously dresses them in their uniform with the medals that they've earned, the emblems of their service, and then puts them on another airplane linked up with a casualty officer escort that takes them home.[5]*

It is a just-the-facts account, but it helps ordinary citizens understand the process and appreciate the honour given to the military's fallen. Jewish families might be similarly assuaged if they knew what happened to their beloved just prior to the burial.

Jewish funeral practices have evolved since ancient times and the precedent-setting funeral in Jewish civilisation is a burial recounted in Genesis

> *And after this, Abraham buried Sarah his wife in the cave of the field of Machpelah before Mamre – the same is Hebron – in the land of Canaan.[6]*

So, forgive me for breaking ranks, and I apologise to those of my own Chevra Kadisha who may feel betrayed, but our community needs to know the process of honouring our dead – not just to demystify the holy work, but to educate. As more and more Jews are opting for cremation, forbidden in traditional Jewish Law [not to speak of its

---

5 The White House, Office of the Press Secretary, October 19, 2017
6 Genesis 23:19

psychic Holocaust associations] my concern is that as swathes of Jews become less engaged with Jewish life, so too they will be less involved with the Jewish way of death. Perhaps if they understood what the Chevra does, they would appreciate a Jewish burial's spiritual value and significance.

Bereft Again

The ritual puts me in a reflective mind. As I dress the woman in her burial shrouds, I wonder about her life: what was important to her, what were her dreams, did she have a happy life, a difficult life? Lying there, this woman is stripped of her history. Was she like the praise-worthy *Eshet Chayil* epitomised in the traditional Friday night paean? Did she rise while it was still night-time, give food to her household and a ration to her maids? Did she spread out her palm to the poor and extend her hands to the destitute? Did she open her mouth with wisdom, and have the teaching of kindness on her tongue? How will I be remembered?

What will her absence mean to those she left behind? As a mother of young children, I drew on the reservoir of my own experiences of being parented. However, now, as a mother of young women in their 20s, I find myself bereft all over again. I am not sure how to be a parent to adults. When my eldest daughter graduated from university, I was so pleased to be able to attend her ceremony. She assumed it was because I was proud of her, and to be sure, that was true. But there was another layer that she could not imagine. I was pleased to be at her graduation so that she did not have to face the public shame of having a dead mother. To this day, I am sorry that I didn't tell my father about my own graduation, denying him the opportunity to enjoy the moment. I told myself I didn't 'believe' in graduations and the pomp of it all. I convinced myself that these ceremonies were meaningless, and that in any event, my father wouldn't understand or be interested. The truth is that I was embarrassed that my mother was dead.

Blessed
and praised
and glorified
and exalted
and extolled
and honoured
and magnified
and lauded be the name
of the Holy One,
blessed be He...

יִתְבָּרַךְ

וְיִשְׁתַּבַּח

וְיִתְפָּאַר

וְיִתְרוֹמַם

וְיִתְנַשֵּׂא

וְיִתְהַדָּר

וְיִתְעַלֶּה

וְיִתְהַלָּל שְׁמֵהּ

דְּיקֻדְשָׁא

בְּרִיךְ הוּא

The Kaddish Cycle

Everyone dies at the end of some counting, long or short...

And the hard words of the Kaddish are like a gun salute

into the bright summer sky

Yehudah Amichai , Israeli poet

I think about death when I wake up in the morning, for I am very grateful to have come through the night unscathed. For this, I say the traditional phrase that starts with the words *Modah Ani Lefanacha* offering gratitude for the return of my soul. Whether the day waiting for me will be exhilarating or fraught, I am grateful that the day is still there for me. That is, of course, as long as I make it to the end of the day without calamity. Three of my days have been forever distorted by death. The first time was in 1980 at home, when my day started with nothing awry but ended with a dead mother. In 1992, the same thing happened. I woke up to a beautiful warm summer's day in New York, but the day ended in winter with the cold body of my dead father. And in 2017, as the morning light of a London day emerged, a phone call from Australia broke the news that my younger brother had dropped dead at the gym a few hours earlier.

There is a tradition that if something happens three times, it is referred to as a *chazaka*, and it is destined to happen that way repeatedly. Does this mean I will never say goodbye to a loved one and I will never be prepared?

When I reflect on the rituals surrounding my parents' deaths, I remember key moments, but I'm not sure that I can recall the whole process. When my mother died, I was too shocked to make any autonomous decisions, and when my father died, I was too sad to argue with anyone about what might have been my 'rights' as a woman in a religious space.

My brother's death was different. One early Sunday in June 2017, just before I was about to head out to the gym, I had a phone call from my sister-in-law in Australia. I noticed several missed calls since 5.30 am.

'...bad news for you...dead...at the gym. Heart attack.' I did not go to the gym that morning.

Shaking on the spot, I couldn't find words other than 'I can't believe it, I can't believe it.' I knew I would have to swing into administrative action and book a ticket to Australia for the funeral. My formative years were in Australia, and it is a wonderful place in many ways but for me, it has been a place tinged with great losses and sadness. With my brother's death, the fate of Australia as doomed territory was now sealed. Suddenly, I was the only one left from my original nuclear family, although like a pruned rose branch, I have grafted and cultivated my own family.

I boarded a flight that evening only to realise that the trouble with flying to Australia is that, generally, it's a flight filled with happy, smiling people, heading there for a holiday, a family reunion or a celebration. I sat there sniffling and felt decidedly out of place for it's a destination brimming with anticipated pleasures and friendliness. In stark contrast, the short flights I regularly take across Europe for my work are filled with busy people in suits, averting a stranger's gaze, with laptops open looking decidedly important and in meeting preparation mode.

This 2017 flight was a deja vu experience, and this only intensified its difficulty. Twenty-five years earlier, while I was living in New York, my brother called me on a Sunday morning to say that our father had suffered a fatal heart attack. I boarded a flight to bury my father after his sudden death. It was surreal then, and continues to feel surreal even now. How can it be that someone in their prime can be randomly plucked from life so cruelly? Mind you, I have had so much experience of it, I feel foolish to keep asking the question.

When I landed in Singapore, my inbox was full of condolence emails, some with vignettes about the help my brother provided those who were now trying to console me. By the time I got to Melbourne, a 'short hop of only 9 hours' as the pilot breezily reminded us, there were many more emails. One friend reminded me that my brother's first foray into communal work was over 30 years earlier with the Melbourne University Jewish Students' Society. I smiled to myself. I was the one who trained and worked as a social worker because I wanted to help people. I scoffed when my brother studied accounting for in my youthful idealism, it symbolised the evils of capitalism. However, the fact is that through all the voluntary assistance he gave to communal organisations and individuals to help them manage their finances, I am sure my brother assisted many more people than I ever did or will do.

First Kaddish

When my brother died, I was older, a little wiser, and determined to stake my ground in the Kaddish cycle, a corrective to compensate for the missed Kaddishes I did not recite for my parents. There are five different types of Kaddish,[7] and over time, I learned more about them. My first Kaddish is the special one reserved just for funerals or the completion of a section of Talmud. I am standing at the graveside. The coffin has been buried, and hundreds of people vie to shovel clods of mud on top. My voice is raspy, my breath is shallow, and I can feel my legs shaking. I can read the words, but I struggle to vocalise them. I peer at the solitary grave – our parents are buried about 12 miles away in the old Springvale Cemetery in Melbourne but there is no

---

7 https://outorah.org/p/4589/

more room. Even now, our parents cannot comfort him in his distress. Lyndhurst is a relatively new cemetery in the Jewish community, so he will have to make fresh acquaintances and, with time, welcome the latest arrivals to ensure they settle in comfortably for eternity.

Traditionally, only men say Kaddish, and this is still the practice in most Orthodox communities. However, according to many rabbinic authorities, it is acceptable for women to say Kaddish. In fact, in an increasing number of Orthodox communities, including in the UK, women are encouraged to say Kaddish. It was clear to my brother's rabbi that we wanted to say Kaddish and he was positively encouraging.

Women's Voices

A body of literature written by women who have shared their experiences saying Kaddish points to many travails from unhelpful rabbis and unwelcoming communities to synagogue architecture and disapproving women congregants who make mourning women reluctant to recite Kaddish. Some women cite this as a trigger for their departure from Orthodoxy.[8]

As it was a late afternoon funeral, we intended to start the *shiva* week (the seven days of mourning) by sitting on low chairs in the funeral hall before nightfall. This made the day of the funeral count as the first day. Because of the vast crowd who had come to bury my brother and the late hour, there was no time to return to the hall from the actual grave, so with typical Melbournian ingenuity, some strong men from the funeral home rushed to bring chairs to the graveside, and we sat down in the warm Melbourne breeze next to the freshly buried coffin to receive our first comforters. I thought of Psalm 137: "By the rivers of Babylon, there we sat down, yea, we wept, when we remembered Zion." And here we sat by the edge of the grave, and wept when we remembered...

---

8 *Kaddish: Women's Voices* Smart, Michal & Ashkenas, Barbara [eds] Urim Publications, 2014 This compilation of 52 essays is a good example, but there are many others.

Kaddish For A Week

The routine becomes familiar to a mourner. I encounter the other four distinct versions of Kaddish that are regularly recited in the synagogue. There is the Half Kaddish (*Chatzi Kaddish* in Hebrew) which is the simplest form of the prayer and is recited as a separation between sections of a prayer unit. There is the Whole Kaddish *(Kaddish Shalem)* recited at the conclusion of the main section a prayer unit. The Rabbis' Kaddish *(Kaddish D'Rabbanan)* recited after a short lecture focussed on a piece of Talmud and the Mourner's Kaddish *(Kaddish Yatom)* both become my companions at various points in the prayer service. Each one has slight variations said during the three daily prayers in the morning, afternoon and evening. Mourners recite both the Rabbi's Kaddish and the Mourner's Kaddish, and so the words are becoming increasingly familiar. The patter is comforting and strangely consoling.

During my *shiva* week in Melbourne, I attended my brother's synagogue for daily services. I was touched by the respect and courtesy shown to me: my brother had been an indispensable lay leader helping to run the synagogue, and the men repeatedly told me how fond they were of him. At the end of each morning prayer service, I sat on a low stool as is customary, and the men filed past me and recited the traditional words of comfort. One man pledged that he would continue to say Kaddish for my brother for the whole year. Everyone dispersed to their daily activities, and I spent the day comforted by scores of friends whom I had not seen for years.

The evening services were said at his home, with lots of visitors and short speeches. A couple of times during the *shiva*, someone came to ask to 'borrow' a few men for a *shiva* in the next street for an elderly person for whom they could not muster the requisite ten men. Whenever we were overwhelmed by the number of visitors, I would think, how much worse would it be to have no visitors.

Making Space for the Mourner

The Friday night service, ushering in the Sabbath, takes place in the synagogue. As I am a mourner, I must wait outside during the singing of the initial part of the service. So I wait in the vestibule with another woman whose elderly mother had died earlier that week. At a particular juncture in the prayer, the congregation stands up, and one of the wardens comes to escort us into the sanctuary. As we walk in, we are greeted with the words said to mourners, 'May God comfort you among all the mourners of Zion and Jerusalem.'

The rabbi gave a short speech in which he reminded the congregation that there were two newly bereaved women in the community and asked the men to recite Kaddish unhurriedly to ensure that the women mourners would not be left behind. Though written in Hebrew letters, the prayer is in Aramaic, and it takes time to get accustomed to the pronunciation. No-one dared utter any objection to the rabbi's request, which was made with sensitivity and tact. I was touched by his handling of our desire to recite Kaddish. It is a testimony that this need is being increasingly acknowledged in many – albeit not in all – Orthodox settings. Kaddish equality is no longer seen as radical, rebellious or eccentric.

In this way, my generation is role-modelling to younger women raising expectations about their ritual engagement levels. Mothers tell their daughters that their voices matter, that their prayers matter, and that refusing a woman the opportunity to say Kaddish denies a woman her place in the community. It denies her right to exist.

Kaddish For Thirty Days

A mourner recites Kaddish for 11 months for parents while for a spouse, child or sibling, the requirement is 30 days. I left Melbourne a couple of days after the end of the *shiva*, and arrived in London at 5.30 am on a Friday morning. I headed to my local synagogue for the regular 7.20 am morning service. There would be no problem at our synagogue as our rabbi encourages women to say Kaddish, and for years, I have been saying Kaddish on the anniversaries of my parents' deaths.

For the rest of that month, I said Kaddish three times a day. In the evenings I was regularly joined by two other women in the community mourning their parents. It was a physically and emotionally draining experience, but it offered solace.

My Favourite Kaddish

My husband and I had a long-standing booking for a three-day visit to our daughter who lives in Israel. Everyone has their favourite Kaddish story, and mine happened during those three days in Be'er Sheva in southern Israel. We were at the Be'er Sheva bus station with a two-hour wait for a connection. Around lunchtime, a portly man exited the mini-market and started soliciting for a minyan, a quorum of ten men needed for communal prayers. He approached my husband, and although initially hesitant, I encouraged him to go in so that I could say the afternoon Kaddish. I asked the portly man if I could say Kaddish. He looked at me in derisive bewilderment.

'Your husband can say it. Come, come in.'

We both entered and between the rows of tinned tuna and dried pasta, a motley gathering came together, and the afternoon prayer was conducted. I stood detached from the men, quietly saying the Kaddish for fear of offending anyone but annoyed with myself that this even concerned me. I was just feeling grateful that no one stopped me or expressed disgust. Don't these men have mothers, wives, daughters, sisters, I thought to myself. Why shouldn't the women of Be'er Sheva, if they want to, access the same mourning rituals as the men?

I thought a lot about our childhood during this month of Kaddish. My brother and I were known as the 'milkbar kids' as we lived on top of our family milkbar [convenience store] in Melbourne. Every day after school we would come home, watch way too much television and then when the lights were out, sneak downstairs to steal chocolates and other treats. Our parents pretended not to notice. In the mornings, Stan the Baker Man would take us on his bread delivery round and en route, drop us off at the nearby primary school. Other kids envied our milkbar lifestyle and for us, it was just a game. Only as a young adult did I begin to understand that running the store was not a game. For our immigrant parents, with limited education and skills who worked selfless 18-hour days, it was survival. They made sacrifices so we could have a more comfortable life.

Growing up, we did not perceive our parents as scarred or their decision to have children as remarkable. Consequently, I was stunned reading Imre Kertész's *Kaddish for an Unborn Child*.[9] Kertész, a Hungarian Holocaust survivor who won the 2002 Nobel Prize for Literature, had his character 'recite' Kaddish for the child he would not bring into the world that had suffered the Shoah. This attitude contradicted everything I knew about survivors who had children and rebuilt their communities, their Holocaust experiences notwithstanding. I was surrounded by survivors who, like my parents, wanted to get as far away from Europe as possible, hence Melbourne's Jewish community grew exponentially in the late 1940s and 1950s. One could say that Melbourne embraced the approach advocated by rabbi-philosopher Emil Fackenheim, who declared the 614th Commandment: not to hand Hitler a posthumous victory – that survival of authentic Jewish life was imperative.[10]

---

9 Kertész, Imre *Kaddish for an Unborn Child*, 1990
10 Fackenheim, Emil *The Jewish Return to History* Jewish tradition counts 613 Commandments both positive and negative.

Second Generation

Much has been written about the 'Second Generation,' the children of survivors and my worldview has certainly been shaped by the aftermath of the Holocaust. Helen Epstein's[11] groundbreaking work gave my generation a voice and legitimated many of our feelings and frustrations. While there is often a lot of focus on the high achieving survivors or those who are traumatized and psychologically paralysed, there is not enough credit for the exceptionally ordinary survivor. These are the people who came to a new country with nothing, worked hard, built a family, put bread on the table and lived a quiet good life, with no animus. These were my parents. My mother after a life in hiding as a child and my father as a concentration camp survivor. They, like the coterie of survivors around them, were exceptional in their ordinariness. In contrast to Kertész, having children was precisely their response to trauma and destruction.

Final Kaddish

Kaddish for a sibling is for 30 days and almost a year later, I am marking the first anniversary of my brother's death, and it feels like a transitional moment. Somehow, I feel like I have to get this particular Kaddish 'right,' and as I say the words, I think not just about my brother, but I also think about how grateful I am for the support of my doting husband and thoughtful daughters. Although I have lived in London for nearly 30 years, it took me many years before I felt it was home. Initially, I felt rootless and disoriented, foreign, unable to read social cues even though I spoke English. With time, I have come to understand these feelings of dislocation as unresolved grief for what I left behind in Australia. I imagined a sort of suspended animation in which my childhood still existed. My family was still intact and my friends remained just as they were growing up, not having established

---

11 Epstein, Helen *Children of Holocaust Survivors*, 1979

lives of their own. For many years, I longed to go back and belong somewhere, to have a place where I mattered.

My Mattering Map

It turned out that I mattered where I was and did not need to be in a faraway land. I am constantly surprised to realise that I have a life and friends in London that have defined my adulthood and continue to sustain me.

Empathy also matters. I think about the daily tragedies that befall innocent people across the world. The fragility of life demands we appreciate what we have. When people ask me how I am, my standard retort is along the lines: 'I woke up this morning, so I'm fine.' This might elicit a nervous laugh, but I genuinely live with an awareness that everything can change with the blink of an eye. This uncertainty shapes my reality. I wish I could tell you it forces me to make every minute count. Alas, I still waste too much time wondering what could have been, or what might still be, not always focusing my gratitude on the wonderful opportunities in front of me.

During that first month, for 30 intense days, I constructed my life around Kaddish. I rushed to the synagogue in the morning, and I rushed home from work with the next Kaddish in mind. A year later, although I had not said Kaddish for several months, I identified with Leon Wieseltier, who in his work simply titled *Kaddish*, wrote movingly about his transition out of a full year of saying it.

> ... *It is my first morning without the Kaddish. Now I am a mourner without an instrument... When the others rise to say Kaddish, I also rise, but I stand silent. I am with them, but I am not of them, I am a mourner on his way out of mourning, a man in the halfway house of grief, whose release from death's company has at last been granted.*

I too feel released, but it is a halfway house where I fear I will have to return.

A Block of Stone

We return to the scene of the crime. Since we were last here, new residents have moved in. It is almost a year since my brother died, and I have returned to Australia for the 'stone-setting' – a short prayer service by the graveside, marking the public show of the deceased's tombstone. Sometimes called the 'unveiling,' in Hebrew the tombstone is called the *matzevah*. In Israel, this ceremony is often held within the first 30 days of the person's death, but in the Diaspora, it's more common towards the end of the first year. We gather again – my sister-in-law and nieces draw on their resilience and love of their husband and father to honour him with dignity. I am grateful for my friends who have come to the cemetery again, demonstrating their unfailing concern and support.

The words of the tombstone are read aloud. It is common to list one's family on the tombstone: devoted father of… beloved wife of… adored son of…cherished daughter of… These facts are the easy part while choosing the epitaph is the challenge. Summing up a person's life in just a few words seems cruel and heartless, a diminishing of their essence, yet it's what we do, and it's what is left for our own future generations, let alone cemetery tourists. Tip: plan in advance. I've been working on my own epitaph for years but I'm still not happy with it.

The service ends, Kaddish is said, and as is customary, people place stones on the grave – symbolically as a marker of permanence and memory. We linger around the tombstone, then slowly walk back to the car park where we all disperse and head home – we have left the world of the dead and return to the world of the living. However, the living carry the dead within them, the ancestors who formed them, those whom they loved, and lost, in real time, and those yet to be born. It is this future that we are commanded to grasp with both hands.

Yahrzeit

The author Sholem Aleichem suggested a unique *yahrzeit* ritual
for his family:

> *At my grave, and throughout a whole year, and then every
> year on the Jahrzeit, my remaining son, and my son-in-law, if
> they are so minded, should say Kaddish after me. And if they
> do not wish to do this, or if they have no time for it, or if it be
> against their religious convictions, they can be absolved from
> this duty only if they all come together with my daughters and
> my grandchildren and with good friends, and read this my will,
> and also select one my stories, one of the really joyous ones and
> read it aloud it whatever language they understand best, and let
> my name be mentioned by then with laughter rather than not be
> mentioned at all.*[12]

My more conventional *yahrzeit* ritual leaves me choked up – *farklempt*
– rather than feeling whimsical like Sholem Aleichem. The *Yahrzeit*
(Yiddish term used by Ashkanazim), or *Nachalah* (Hebrew term used
by Sephardim), is marked on the anniversary of the death, according
to the Jewish calendar. I anticipate an emotionally punishing three-
week period in which I will commemorate the deaths of my mother,
father and brother. Privately, it is a day of personal reflections and
customs that might include lighting a memorial candle at home, recit-
ing psalms, offering charity, and visiting the deceased's grave. Publicly,
the *yahrzeit* requires a minyan to recite Kaddish. It can also be the
occasion to share the deceased's story publicly, for the *yahrzeit* bridges
private sorrow and communal performance, the world of the dead and
the living.

I orchestrate my *yahrzeit* plans months in advance as I must get to the
synagogue in the evening and the morning. I clear my diary of any
travel, decline late work meetings, and forego early morning gym.
Living in London, sadly I cannot visit their graves in Melbourne,
but I do have photos of their tombstones, and I spend time looking at

---

12 *New York Times, Wed, May 17, 1916*

the few old family photos I have, re-reading teenage diaries, trying to reconstruct the lives of those I can no longer question.

Yizkor and Shame

In addition to the annual *yahrzeit*, the *Yizkor* remembrance prayer is recited liturgically four times a year: Passover, Shavuot, Yom Kippur, and Shemini-Atzeret. The prayer is typically recited in synagogue though it may be said at home.

In many Diaspora synagogues, parented-people leave the sanctuary during the *Yizkor* memorial prayer. When I was much younger, I sensed glances of pity. As a newly-wed and young mother, well-intentioned friends rattled off advantages to not having living parents, such as not facing criticism over my parenting style or having to choose between my mother-in-law or mother's Passover seder table. However, in recent years, as we age, more of my friends remain inside the synagogue during the service, for they too have joined the ranks of the bereaved. My heart now aches for the young men and women who remain in the synagogue, often those in their late teens or early 20s who have lost a parent to illness. I see myself in their downcast eyes, averting attention.

I think I've been what D.W. Winnicott, the English paediatrician and psychoanalyst, calls a 'good enough' mother to my girls, but I'm not sure if I've been a 'good enough' daughter. My husband's parents also died when he was young, [but that's another story] and now, 40 years later, I find myself apologising for not having ageing parents to worry about, not having an irritating mother-in-law to take to the doctors, a father losing his memory walking around the neighbourhood in his pyjamas, a mother crippled by arthritis, or father-in-law with a cancerous prostate.

The Vacuum of Absent Parents

As a motherless daughter, I couldn't empathise with my friends who complained about their mothers. I just wanted them to be quiet. But now, as my adult friends look to me for some empathy, I fear I don't have enough to give. If they forget my story, they say to me, 'you know how it feels to look after old parents,' and I have to say, 'actually, I don't know how it feels.' I think of the children orphaned by tsunamis and earthquakes, natural disasters disrupting natural family life, and I wonder about a generation of young men and women who will parent their children without their elders to guide them.

Ageing parents protect you from thoughts of early death. While I live with a powerful feeling that death is just around the corner, if you have an 80-year-old parent, it's perfectly reasonable to be focussed on their end and not your own. Deprived of the chance to look after my parents in their old age, I find myself bitter that I have also been cheated of the opportunity to shine as the dutiful daughter I always wanted to be. While I can't huddle with other women venting frustrations and confidences about their parents, I can warn them that they cannot begin to imagine the looming vacuum awaiting them when their parents are no longer.

How will my children learn to look after me when they're older if they have never seen me look after anyone else? Most children practice grieving over their grandparents as they learn the etiquette from a dignified burial of an elderly relative. It is a comparatively commonplace experience that they can talk about with friends. My children, now in their 20s, are in for a shock.

Despite apparent maturity and a mortgage, you're still not ultimately responsible for yourself until your parents are dead. I have often wondered what it is like to be a 50-year-old child-adult. I haven't been someone's child for so long that it's difficult to imagine.

I have no burdensome responsibilities, no-one anxiously waiting for me to phone them every day, no byzantine medical bureaucracy to negotiate, no resentment at having to put my career on hold to look after a doddering parent, no forced Sunday lunch visits, no extra payments for nursing care and no arguments with my spouse about our parents' care.

Therein lies my conflicted emotions and guilty secret: being parent-free, I am sad a little bit every day, but there are times when it feels like a relief.

...though He be high above all blessings, hymns, praises and consolations uttered in the world – and say: Amen.

לְעֵלָּא

מִן־כָּל־בִּרְכָתָא

וְשִׁירָתָא

תֻּשְׁבְּחָתָא

וְנֶחָמָתָא,

דִּי־אֲמִירָן בְּעָלְמָא.

וְאִמְרוּ: אָמֵן.

אָמֵן

Hearts and Heroes

Intensive care is a foreign country – not one I would recommend visiting. Yet I found myself there on the Jewish New Year 5778 (September 2017), slowly waking in a disorientated stupor. With tentative steps and rather impressive scars, I made it home for Yom Kippur, the holiest day of the year. My brother's death prompted me to seek medical advice which proved I was next in line. Ergo, as I underwent a quadruple bypass, I understood that posthumously, my brother saved my life.

The haunting High Holy Day prayer *Unetaneh Tokef* had been ringing in my ears for days:

> *"On Rosh Hashanah, it is inscribed, and on Yom Kippur, it is sealed – how many shall pass away and how many shall be born, who shall live and who shall die..."*

The skilled surgeon explained that he would be breaking my breastbone in two halves to access my heart. I would be like the heifer, the goat and the ram, each split in half to create an everlasting covenant between God and Abraham.[13] But my covenant would be with my friends: while my breastbone temporarily lay bare my heart so that it could be physically healed, it also allowed the exposed heart to absorb the bountiful messages of kindness and compassion my family and I received. While magnificent steel stitches attest to the breastbone being perfectly realigned, the little swollen bumps are the feelings of affection and tenderness for my well-being that could not be contained.

---

13 Genesis 15: 9-10

We all build a narrative about our lives – one that if repeated often enough, we actually plan for. Mine was quite straightforward – I would die young. It would be quick and it would be tragic. I based this narrative on the early and sudden deaths of my parents. Even though I blamed the Nazis for their heart attacks, and I had not gone through such health-compromising experiences, I was convinced it would happen to me.

And then the unexpected happened. My younger brother dropped dead and suddenly it became his narrative and not mine. Shortly afterward, following consultations with a cardiologist and a barrage of tests that discovered significantly blocked arteries, I was lying in intensive care after quadruple bypass surgery. This upgrade to my heart has given me, according to my doctors, at least 15 years before I may need a replacement or a tweak. 'You're only as old as your heart,' the surgeon genially noted. 'So think of it as a new beginning.' If only I could start my whole life all over again, I think to myself, how would I want it to be different?

Who Will Live and Who Will Die?

Of course, I cannot assume that I am now safe – each year we stand on the *Unetaneh Tokef* precipice. Those expecting a birth wait anxiously that all will be well, and those anticipating a loss wait fretfully for the year's events to unfold. It would be churlish to ask for too much happiness as we try to keep unexpected and unspeakable miseries at bay. Yet *Unetaneh Tokef* is not about individual fate alone – fires, floods, earthquakes, plague, and hunger entangle personal experiences with that of the collective. Our destiny is tied up with that of our community, the wider Jewish world, and indeed of humanity.

Since my heart operation, I feel an even greater burden to make meaning of my life. To squander this gift would insult my brother's memory, for his sacrifice gave me the window of opportunity to lengthen my days. While I have always tried to make each day matter, I have never before been more assiduously committed to doing so.

The Talmud suggests that the world was created for my sake. There is a task in this world that only I, and I alone, can carry out.
Rav Abraham Isaac Kook would contextualise my life thus: When I was not yet formed, I was of no worth; that I did not yet exist meant that there was no need for me to exist. However, now that I have been formed, there must be a reason for my being: a mission that only I can accomplish.

Fearing My Potential

Consequently, my existence is of crucial importance, not just for myself but for all of humanity and the entire universe. The thought troubles me. How could it be that the world hangs in the balance according to the pre-ordained task that I must fulfill. What if I can't work out what that task is? And if the smile I gave the lonely person I walked past in the park this morning was my task, then I guess my hours left are numbered.

Taking a leaf from theologian Abraham Joshua Heschel, I fear life perhaps more than death. I dread squandering my life and I feel an indebtedness to make it meaningful. I fear wasting time on the frivolous, not fulfilling my potential or even worse, the terror that I might never identify my potential. "Our goal should be to live life in radical amazement... get up in the morning and look at the world in a way that takes nothing for granted. Everything is phenomenal; everything is incredible; never treat life casually. To be spiritual is to be amazed," Heschel preached.

I am not a jealous person by nature. However, I envy those who meet Heschel's yardstick.

More than that, I envy those who know how to enjoy their holidays; those who can dance with wild abandon at a wedding. I envy people who see the good in the world. I might think that they are naïve and a little simple – but I envy them, for they are not afraid of life. I do not have great material demands, but I do want more time. I don't mean the time we all want – another hour in the day to finish off a work project, a few more minutes to relax in the bath, a weekend away with some friends to recharge one's batteries. I mean serious time – time in the future to help my daughters choose their wedding dress, time to babysit for my grandchildren and dance at their weddings. I think about the time stolen from my parents and their missed opportunities. I replay an imaginary scene in my head. My daughter is getting married in Israel. My father, not a man prone to public speaking, would stand up to give a short speech. 'If you would have told me,' he starts to say, 'when I was in Auschwitz, that I would live to see my grandchild getting married in the State of Israel, I would have told you that you're crazy!' There would be knowing smiles, a few tears and much joy.

For years I worried that I would not have this sort of time – my narrative begrudged me the possibility of wedding dresses and grandchildren. And now, things have changed and with an upgraded heart I have to create a new narrative that says I'm likely to be around for quite a while. They may not be saying Kaddish for me so soon after all.

The Burden of a Legacy

And that's a real problem because now I am compelled to leave a legacy that is way beyond my immediate family – I want to know that I have done the most I could on this earth – the most for my family, for my community and the whole wide world. That's because, despite my very dark view of the world, I still carry embers of naivety from youth, when, much to the horror of my parents I gave up an offer to study law at university to study social work instead, because, oh, I am so embarrassed to admit it, but in classic Second Generation behaviour, I wanted to help people.

Readers might wonder, 'who does this woman think she is? Why does she think she's so important that she has to leave a legacy?' Well, let me counterpose this question: 'What makes you think you're not important?' Why doesn't everyone think that they have a responsibility to do something remarkable with their lives? As we breathe, we have a singular obligation to make life meaningful by the sheer virtue of being alive. A core value in Judaism is Tikkun Olam – to perform acts of kindness that perfect or repair our damaged world. It is everyone's duty.

The Love of Friendship

As word got out about my surgery, I was overcome by everyone's concern and heartfelt compassion. Although over the years I have participated in meal rotas, picked up someone else's kids and dropped off some shopping, now that it was my turn to accept help, I felt vulnerable and exposed, incapacitated physically, but also on emotional overdrive to sustain the onslaught of thoughtfulness. We should all be blessed with the challenges of accepting people's kindness.

Friends who tell me they love me make me cry, an email that says 'don't die, you matter to me' takes my breath away, a text message telling me 'you are too precious to lose' melts my resolve. I am surprised by how moved I am by the countless requests for my Hebrew name so that I can be included in other people's prayers.

If we are lucky, we are safe in the knowledge that we are essential to our family and friends, but when it's articulated, when those invisible bonds of friendship are made very concrete, it becomes humbling, precious and terrifying. What did I do to deserve such powerful, embracing friendships? And do I have the qualities necessary to be a good enough friend in return?

We are obligated to show *hakarat hatov*, gratitude, for all that we receive. Yet, in my circumstances, a simple thank you seems inadequate. However, for now, I am learning that this must be enough. Sharing my vulnerability and thanking someone for their help acknowledges that I am incomplete, and for this too, I must be grateful. "Either friendship or death, as one who has no friends, is better off dead," Reva teaches in the Talmud.[14] Without my wonderful friendships, my heart might still be beating, but a part of me would certainly have died.

And so, on Yom Kippur shortly after my surgery, I force myself to stand despite the pain and, as ritual requires, gently beat my heart at every sin of the Yom Kippur *Viddui* confession. Each sin hurt me sharply, for the scar on my heart is still tender.

Ever since, my knobbled scar serves as a reminder that nothing is certain and death is merely a heartbeat away.

14 Taanit 23a:17

יְהֵא שְׁלָמָא רַבָּא
מִן-שְׁמַיָּא,
וְחַיִּים עָלֵינוּ
וְעַל-כָּל-יִשְׂרָאֵל.

וְאִמְרוּ אָמֵן.

May there be abundant peace
from heaven,
and life for us
and all Israel

– and say: Amen.

Death in a Pandemic

I miss my Sunday morning routine. Gym, newspapers, cemetery. It's my Chevra Kadisha day, and I'm on duty, waiting for the text informing me what time to turn up to prepare the body for a funeral later that day. However, the 2020 Coronavirus upended our routines. It brought protracted, sometimes fatal illness, unemployment, families fractured, mental health compromised and closed international borders. And when lockdown was announced, the Chevra Kadisha instructed those over 70 and/or at high risk, to stay home. So I was furloughed - my bypass surgery rendered me vulnerable, and I must await new instructions for when I can zip up the motorway to the cemetery.

The pandemic will be defined by how we lived online and will inevitably be remembered for how we mourned online. All the routines of death went awry. Technology was deployed at every ritual turn: while funerals were live-streamed, online *shiva* visits became de rigueur, and rabbis debated whether an online prayer service constituted a halachic minyan to say Kaddish. The Yahrzeit, the annual anniversary when many seek the comfort of a minyan to say Kaddish, even if they are not regular shul-goers, was suspended in many places.

Robbed of Rites

And what of the deceased? They were also bereft: with no send-off, no last family embrace, no chance for the last word and no friend to hold their hand. Pending regulations at various times, some people were buried alone with only their gravediggers for company; thus, a bereft family's pain was amplified.

And the body that must be prepared for burial? Sadly, those who died of Covid-19 were robbed of the traditional *taharah*. Communities worldwide adapted procedures as dictated by the laws of their country. In some places, those who died of Covid-19 were placed directly into a coffin with the *tachrichim* shrouds placed on top. Elsewhere, a modified *taharah* took place. In still other locales, a complete *taharah* in hazmat suits was possible.

While cremation is a central tenet of some religions, Jewish law opposes cremation, although of course, some Jews choose that option. Cremation was in the spotlight during Covid-19 as certain countries mandated it in order to stop the virus from spreading. The UK government tried to mandate cremation for all Covid-19 victims. However, Jewish and Muslim organizations successfully lobbied the government to respect the religious traditions of those opposed to cremation.

I have a visceral reaction against cremation, no doubt influenced by my family's experience of the Holocaust and reinforced by my Chevra experience. It feels that cremation denies the body its transition to a burial place that brings their earthly journey to a natural end. However the fact that cremation is an increasingly popular option for families means that communal and religious leaders need to understand the motivation and perceived attraction of cremation if they hope to reverse this trend.

Death during Corona has its added complexities. While I have a low level of anxiety about succumbing to its ravages, it is a background worry. Like so many who are separated from their families, it pains me to think of my daughters who live abroad, unable to visit me in my last days, and with limited air travel, unable to attend my funeral. I am fixated on this because I was abroad when my father and my brother died – with no warning, they were dead, and I had to scramble to catch a flight to get back to Australia as soon as possible. But this was before Corona, and I console myself that I was there for their respective funerals.

Death is the Only Conversation

Death in the time of Corona has catapulted mortality into the public arena. Funeral directors, gravediggers, morgue operators and those managing the death bureaucracy have been featured in the media. Websites such as Death Over Dinner[15] and Death Salon[16] bring people together for a facilitated conversation about death. The Shomer Collective[17] is a similar, but more expansive initiative in the Jewish community. The virtual Good Grief Festival[18] attracted thousands of viewers and numbers swelled in the popular Facebook groups discussing death. Corona accentuated loneliness in the community and also gave us permission to acknowledge our deepest fears surrounding mortality in a publicly acceptable way. People wanted to talk about their grief, almost as part of an initiation into a sacred fraternity. Corona might kill you in an abnormal way, but it is helping to normalise the conversation around death.

Everyone will have their corona stories: thankfully mine are mundane and no-one in my immediate family has been sick. While I've stayed in touch with friends via WhatsApp and look forward to meeting in a coffee shop again, basically I've adapted to lockdown and limited social interactions surprisingly well. However, I have found it increasingly difficult to concentrate: my mind drifts, I flitter between tasks and I flick between Netflix shows before any first scene is finished. The plague atmosphere has its internal contradictions. I have a constant low-level of anxiety about the future: on the one hand this paralyses me because I can't focus, and on the other hand this galvanises me into action with the mantra 'if not now, when?' ringing in my ears.

---

15   https://deathoverdinner.org
16   https://deathsalon.org
17   https://www.shomercollective.org
18   https://goodgrieffest.com

Covid has sharpened the fear we all have about our mortality, whether we have acknowledged it or not. I'm taken back to the Second World War and to my parents torn from their families. Their lives were upended and they were left with barely any documentation to prove their existence. My mind always takes me back to the War. I visualise being ripped from my daughters and cannot fathom the loss. Sometimes, I dread the act of feeling. Once emotionally invested in something, the thought of loss becomes too hard to bear. So, it seems easier not to feel too deeply. Does that make me a coward or a pragmatist?

Chevra Kadisha in the Spotlight

In March 2021, the United Synagogue Chevra Kadisha won the UK Jewish community's 2020 Volunteer Team of the Year Charity Award. This recognition of their work was well-deserved, particularly given the challenges of Corona, but paradoxically, threw them into the spotlight in a way that is contrary to their fundamental tenet of being anonymous.

Clearly, that playbook has now been rewritten: a Chevra Kadisha is taken for granted until it doesn't exist. While large communities with a functioning religious infrastructure will ensure its members are buried according to Jewish tradition, what of dwindling, or less affiliated communities? We have to know about the Chevra Kadisha and its work needs to be protected, publicly appreciated and understood.

However, we are at risk: despite the money poured into Jewish education and Jewish cultural initiatives, there's concern about the swathes of young Jewish people who are not particularly engaged with Jewish life. I'm afraid that there's no reason to think that they will be particularly engaged with Jewish death. As unpopular as it sounds, younger people need to understand that the business of burial and cemetery maintenance will be part of their future communal obligation.

So post-Covid, what lies over the horizon? The physical act of *taharah* will be fully reinstated and will always remain a constant - it is impossible to even imagine that this rite would ever be willingly abandoned. However, hybrid mourning may emerge as the preferred option for some families including a small, intimate funeral live streamed, an in-person *shiva* of one or two days with the rest of the week comprised of online condolence visits, and Kaddish online recited from the comfort of one's home, and with a 'community' scattered around the world. These post-Corona adaptations may also change the ways we collect stories of the deceased or give family time and space to build a legacy of solace and reminiscences.

עֹשֶׂה שָׁלוֹם בִּמְרוֹמָיו הוּא יַעֲשֶׂה שָׁלוֹם עָלֵינוּ, וְעַל־כָּל־יִשְׂרָאֵל וְאִמְרוּ אָמֵן.

He who makes peace in high places, may He make
peace for us and for all Israel: and say Amen.

Life After Death

It's on me. In our family, death is my responsibility and it's a big job. Who to notify first? Updating our wills. Which rabbi to consult? Where are all the passwords stored? What happens if my husband and I die together in a plane crash? What's the password to the passwords? What about that envelope of cash I've got stored away that no-one else knows about? And if I die suddenly, who is going to tidy up before everyone arrives to pay a *shiva* call? The Swedish call it Death Cleaning, but I call it my untamed fear and I'm trying to get it under control. In the meantime, I think about the burdens I will leave behind.

Life-After

I'm not so worried about my own 'after-life' – rather, I'm more concerned about my daughters' 'life-after' I'm gone. What sort of memory bank have I created for them? How will they remember me? Have I made them resilient? Was that even my responsibility?

Life-After for my daughters will inevitably involve stuff, those accoutrements attesting to the ordinariness of the everyday such as books, clothes, photos, gadgets and jewellery. They will be surrounded by felled trees: bank statements, articles that I haven't read, notebooks, drafts of articles I've not finished writing, passports and post-it notes. During my 20s, I kept long lists of what I'd done each year: books read, theatre seen, travel, courses taken, thinking that activities meant achievements. I also chronicled my angst-ridden failures in long, rambling diary entries. This cache sits in a plastic bag, hidden in a cardboard box, concealed in a cloth bag, secreted behind some T-shirts in my cupboard. I haven't looked at what I wrote for years, and although, Kafka-like, I think about burning them, I can't bring myself to do it as it feels like an act of self-mutilation. I wonder if they could be buried with me?

After my mother died, nothing was moved from her cupboard and her dresses hung in suspended animation for 13 years till my father died. Then it was time to empty our family home and clear out the remnants of their lives. I wanted nothing, save for the photos and a few documents such as my parents' Australian naturalisation papers. Boxes of clothes, furniture, kitchen goods, beddings and towels were distributed between various charities. I didn't flinch for a moment in giving them away, not a shred of sentimentality or regret. Many years later, I just stare at my own stuff, wanting to will it away, but the stuff remains, inanimate and unforgiving. Will my daughters forgive me for the mess I'm leaving them?

My Digital After-Life

I'm writing this as the UK is slowly, but hopefully, emerging from the pandemic. I have had all my vaccinations and staff can choose to return to their offices. Entertainment venues are slowly starting to re-open. I turned 60 during this period, and although it's irrational, I feel like my life is drawing to a close.

Like a responsible parent, I've written my will, disbursing my worldly goods to family members and charities. But what values have I left in my will? Which stories about me will be remembered by my children, and by my friends? What will those stories tell of my humanity? While some people have been able to retrace their family stories from a cache of letters or diaries found in the attic, I have barely anything. However, I want my children and grandchildren to have something in the future and so I am creating a digital archive with relevant information.

There will be photos: my father when he arrived in Australia, my parents' wedding photos, my children's school reports and a few documents. Perhaps it is a testament to the relative stability of my life so far that I can even think of creating such a system. I will add the articles I have written over the years for admittedly, I write for the fleeting rush of immortality, and while doing so, the adrenaline that gives me the feeling that I'll live forever.

Ultimately, all this is really for my future grandchildren: those I may meet, but more so, those whom I fear I will never meet. But I am sadder that they may not meet me. Not because I hope I'll be some sort of super granny, but because I will just be. I will just be in their lives. I will just be a part of their story. I will just be a part of their childhood memories. But if they do not meet me, I will not be.

The Final Mask

I appreciate that it sounds irrational and possibly even ungrateful, to be preparing for one's own demise while being ostensibly healthy and active. But I am driven by the obvious: everything can change in a moment. Hence, while the digital afterlife that I'm curating may sound bizarre and self-indulgent, it's helping me face the closure of my life. There may be a physical chaos when I'm gone, but I owe my children some semblance of online order in my death. In planning these digital memories, I have the rare opportunity while still alive to curate and bequeath the remembrance of things past.

Eventually, I will lie on that metal slab. The women of the Chevra Kadisha will tenderly prepare my body for burial. All the masks that I have worn throughout my life will now be discarded and the final mask will be placed on my face. The strings will be wound behind my ears and then brought together in a bow under my neck to hold it in place. As the women carefully place me in the coffin, what stories will they imagine? What stories will I be able to tell from beyond the grave?

Soon I'll be 20 years older than my mother was when she died, and yet, even with my refurbished heart, I am exhausted from the knowledge that life can end at any moment, in an instant. I cannot fathom the inexplicable: why did I merit so many extra years beyond my mother?

My youngest daughter recently told me that she never uses the phrase 'my grandmother' in conversation with her friends. Instead, she only ever refers to her absent and abstract grandmother as 'my mother's mother.' I fear that her children may say the same thing about me.

Questions to Consider

I hope this book helps you to start the difficult conversations about death with the people who are important in your life. Perhaps you'd like to read this book with a group of friends, maybe you're a teacher who could assign it for a class focussed on Jewish death rites, or you're responsible for training clergy and may find this a useful resource as part of their pastoral care training. And if you belong to a Chevra Kadisha, it would be so helpful to know if my words resonate with some of your experiences. These questions may prove useful in guiding your discussion regarding each section.

My Burial

1. Can you bear to contemplate what happens to your body after your death?

2. How might it be helpful to know the processes of the Chevra Kadisha?

3. Have you made your wishes clear, to the appropriate people, about how you would like to be buried?

Funerals Denied

1. How much do you know about your own parents' or grandparents' lives? And of their deaths? What could you do to find out more?

2. The role of Righteous Gentiles during the Holocaust was very specific. However, are there people who have unconditionally helped your loved ones and deserve some sort of recognition?

3. How do we begin to reconstruct our lives after trauma?

Joining the Chevra

1. If you belong to a Chevra, what motivated you to join, and at what age?

2. What might stop you joining a Chevra?

3. How does death make you think about life?

The Kaddish Cycle

1. What is the attitude towards women saying Kaddish in your community? If you are a woman, how do you feel about saying Kaddish?

2. Have you discussed burial and mourning rites with your parents, siblings and children?

3. How do you feel during the Yizkor service in the synagogue?

Hearts and Heroes

1. How has illness impacted on your sense of mortality?

2. Are you fulfilling your potential? Do you even know what it is?

3. Have you told your friends how important they are to you? Who will miss you when you die?

Death in a Pandemic

1. How did Covid-19 impact your own sense of mortality?

2. What changed in your community regarding mourning rituals during this period? What might be the impact of these changes in the long-term?

3. The Chevra Kadisha was thrust into the spotlight in many places – how did you react to this?

Life After Death

1. Who does the Death Cleaning in your home?

2. How will your legacy be defined? Who will define it?

3. What are your plans to deal with your digital footprint?

4. What stories will be told about you?

Your Answers, Your Experiences

This book was written to encourage more understanding about the work of the Chevra Kadisha and related issues.

I am interested in compiling a series of essays reflecting on personal experiences and would be very happy to hear from you. I also welcome hearing from those with experiences from another faith tradition.

If you would like to contribute to a wider conversation, please email me at sally@sallyberkovic.com